METAMORPHOSIS
Of You

KENNETH JAMES

A process of transformation from an immature form to an adult form

True to life experiences, it's not what you go through, it's how you go through it.

ISBN: 9798623406729
Copyright © 2020 by Kenneth James
All rights reserved. This book or any portion thereof may not be reproduced or used in any manner whatsoever without the express written permission of the publisher except for the use of brief quotations in a book review.

Printed in the United States of America

First Printing, 2020

Interior Design by Indigo Herald

INTRODUCTION

I must say that everything that I've gone through has made me the person I am today. There is something to be said about tough times, uncomfortable circumstances, and adverse filled situations. It is my belief that you can never say what you would do in a certain situation until you find yourself in that place. These are the moments in our lives that shape, mold, and build our character. Your character represents the real you. The you, which surfaces when pressure is applied and causes you to experience emotions that makes you uncomfortable. *It is at that very moment growth has presented you an opportunity*. Confucius once said, "An inconvenience is an unrecognized opportunity."

You see, for some of us there are a certain set of obstacles we must overcome for growth and maturity to flourish. Some respond quickly, while others find it more difficult surrendering to the process. When you are open enough to first, look at self, your perception will lead you in the right direction. It will make the difference in you moving forward and not letting the mistake seem bigger than the opportunity it presented. When you change the way you look at things, the things you look at, change.

Many of these poems / short stories were written by me as I sat in a jail cell. *In the natural I was arrested, but spiritually, I was rescued.* Deep inside I knew the mistakes I made; however, I was not prepared for where they would lead me. When you find yourself in a sequestered position, most often, it is not by accident. It has been my experience that God will allow some things to happen in our lives but that does not mean He caused them. Our actions and decisions carry a heavy penalty. *The only true measure of an action is its' consequence.* I've learned to never look back in regret. Looking back makes you wish you did something different but reflecting lets you know; it made a difference.

Kenneth James,
Circa 2003

Table of Contents

Courage to Live..6

Because of the Adversity..7

Other Side of Agony..8

Unseen Forces..9

Sign of the Times..10

A Soul Mate..11

Just the Way it Goes...12

The Love of Me in You..13

Tried By Fire...14

The Good that Pain Can Do..15

And I Have You...16

Something New..17

Stepping Stone...18

Imagine..19

Carry Me Away...20

Fence I Straddled...21

The Best is Yet to Come...22

Riches Money Cannot Buy...23

Reaching for the Top..24

Nothing to Lose..25

Happiness..26

Crossroad..27

Now I Know..28

This Thing Called Life...29

COURAGE TO LIVE

I guess most people would say I blew my best shot,

I must admit I've come from behind way more times than not.

It's all too familiar to me that the odds outweigh the stack,

There's nothing left now but memories of time I wished I had back.

I can't say for sure that it would be any different than before,

They say you have to hit the bottom and sometimes go even lower.

No one knows your calling is what people fail to see,

This wasn't just a journey but a path toward your destiny.

Something needed to change, I couldn't tell which way to go,

This wasn't the real me, in fact, it's somebody I don't even know.

It's so obvious to me now this emptiness in my soul,

Any sincere desire I had to fill it now, was growing cold.

The flame still flickers on, only much deeper within my spirit,

If only I could just grab it, it's so close now I can hear it.

The daylight is shining brighter, it seems like more than ever,

Each day is a gift that I have learned to treasure.

If you're down and out in despair with nothing left to give,

In your darkest, most desperate moment,

is where you find, the courage to live.

BECAUSE OF THE ADVERSITY

For so long I lived two lives, walking through life without picking sides.

Trying to forget the tracks I traced, hoping the awful truth could somehow be erased.

I can't help myself, so I pray that God would lift me above this someday.

If you never open your eyes you'll never see, this is not supposed to be a mystery.

But we carry on not knowing, that where we're headed, we shouldn't be going.

When you find yourself in a crisis, somewhere down the line there were no sacrifices.

And you can't move on not even a bit, the longer you carry the past the heavier it gets.

It confines you to a space you don't know, it keeps you holding on when you should let go.

Even though it's killing you inside, God will take and use it to make you wise.

Some people never figure it out, so they continue drifting in doubt.

Always wandering down the wrong path,

reaching for something not meant for them to have.

Searching, but never coming to that inner voice deep inside leading you to you.

There must at some point be growth in our hearts because of the adversity.

OTHER SIDE OF AGONY

So how is it that by now I'm still not liberated?

I thought keeping an open mind could not be confiscated.

As it turns out it's true, we all face troubled times,

To stay on the safe side, you must walk a very thin line.

Consequently, I'm confused, this part wasn't in the script,

But it's in my favor, apparently the scales have been tipped.

It's not about what we say, we will all one day be tested,

If you're not relying on God, doesn't matter where your faith rested.

The gray areas of life are highlighted to show,

You can't trust Him with your own know-how; You learn this as you go.

Somehow the thing that's broken surfaces to light,

Because there's no way to fix wrong without doing something right.

What you should've done you didn't and it's hard for you to face,

The results of what you did do seem impossible to embrace.

I've tried to see it clearly, but it remains to baffle me,

Ecstasy often lies on the other side of agony.

UNSEEN FORCES

Gust of wind so fierce and strong,

Blows me in the direction that's wrong.

Destruction so great that's broad and long,

Searching desperately to find my way home.

As I begin to fight in the mist of my struggle,

It's only ruins that remain in the rubble.

Thoughts in my mind of the one I love,

Come and go as clouds that hover above.

You fill me up from the inside out,

Your beauty has taught me what loves all about.

My soul is washed, my spirit renewed,

Your presence in my life, the reason I'm subdued.

I don't believe that there's any greater force,

Then the one we've shared God being the source.

My pride is gone, my ego beat, the past has revealed the smell of defeat.

As I press forward, the desires of my heart,

The sense of urgency lifts me from the dark.

The passion, love, and gentleness you've always shown

Steadies the beat of my heart and ultimately led me home.

The result of my struggle, the weight of a thousand horses,

It's clear now, that I've always been at the mercy of unseen forces.

SIGN OF THE TIMES

Like sands passing through an hourglass,

The afflictions we face are sure to pass.

Patience comes but in due time,

Conflicts that arise are just another sign.

We've hindered ourselves all too often,

Through much discomfort our hearts are softened.

Sufferings we endure are to help us see,

Such lessons we must learn so costly.

Decisions we've made, though not in vain,

There's nothing you can lose without some kind of gain.

Day to day life and all that it brings,

Overcoming by perseverance trumps all things.

Reminiscent of the times when things were not good,

To change what's taken place, I only wished I could.

Consequences of our actions reach to the skies,

Letting go of what's behind, time to say our good-byes.

Inner peace comes from within, this we all must find,

Knowing what's behind the scenes, is just a sign of the times.

A SOUL MATE

There is only one that's meant for me,

To come into my heart and set it free.

To unlock the love that's trapped within,

To watch how it blossomed into everlastin.

To know that even though we've been apart,

To carry you in the very center of my heart.

To walk through this life holding hands,

To leave a footprint of love marked in the sands.

To make a promise that this will always last,

To carve it in stone and never have to ask.

To believe that we transcend what's behind,

To know this is one of the best you'll ever find.

To never have to worry, it is you that I trust,

To realize that she is oh, so marvelous.

To share ups and downs, is what it's all about,

To know I truly love you without a shadow of a doubt.

To take time and to make sure everything is okay,

To tell the one you love, don't ever go away.

To want you with me is something I'll always keep,

To treasure you so deeply, it's too good to even to speak.

So who is that one to whom I always relate,

That one is you for me, my soul mate.

JUST THE WAY IT GOES

Take a second and imagine if our paths had never crossed,

What would it be that you wished your heart never felt or lost?

Because if I could do it all again, I'd tear down every wall

And remove every rough spot that ever caused us to fall.

So long I treaded through the waters for oh so many days,

Swimming my way through life, but now I'm surfing the waves.

There's a time for every man, to find the road that's straight,

The one he thought was a dead end, held the key that opened the gate.

When we gamble on life and lose, we pay way more than it cost,

If you lose the one you love, then love the one you lost.

Some truths are only realized when it's just you all alone,

When people you thought you'd always have one day, suddenly are gone.

Be careful how you perceive, things aren't always as they appear,

When you can't see it as being real, you've given in to your fear.

Despite the challenges you face, you're still able to stand strong,

The strength is deep down within, God put it there, hold on.

Where this road leads is an ending only God knows,

Things don't happen by accident, that's just the way it goes.

THE LOVE OF ME IN YOU

If I could see inside you, I'd protect you from your cares,

If love had wings and flew away, we'd walk heaven stairs.

If certain things touch your heart, they also have touched mine,

As our love grows, we learn true love is hard to find.

When you feel as if you can't make it through,

It's at that very moment I realize I'm lost without you.

If ever you find yourself doubting how you feel,

Because we've walked the same path this love remains still.

When life has tested you, and questioned where you stand,

One thing will never change, we'll always be hand and hand.

If time did not exist, we could capture this moment forever,

Remove the space between us and lock our hearts together.

If a rainbow suddenly appears just out of the clear blue,

It wasn't your imagination, it was the love of me in you.

TRIED BY FIRE

I remember right at first you and I were quite a pair

Not knowing what the future, held love was in the air.

All the trust you showed I still couldn't see

As I look back now you loved unconditionally.

I took for granted so much today, I wonder why

We had it oh so good now our ships were passing by.

Nights by the fireplace and snuggles on the sofa,

These times so precious, were meant to bring us closer.

There's often much time for me to contemplate,

It's never been any clearer you'll always be my perfect mate.

I've searched and searched so far even the depths of my soul

It was you being there, that sheltered me from the cold.

This sometimes lonely road filled with questions and pain,

We made it through it all, even the heavy fog and rain.

You believed in me when I didn't know where I belong,

You loved me sincerely, I'm so glad you sang that song.

Only God could have shown me this was heavenly,

I didn't know it then, but you were my perfect melody.

Our love survived the toughest times, our calling is even higher,

It never failed not even once, when it was tried by fire.

THE GOOD THAT PAIN CAN DO

I sometimes think to myself too much damage has been done,

I can't change what has happened, so a new chapter has begun.

If I could lose it, I did, I tried with all due respect,

Through it all, it was me He was trying to perfect.

What's ahead is unsure, it won't be easy that's a fact,

No longer will I allow what others do; dictate how I act.

You think you know yourself well that much may be true,

Sometimes pain is what it takes to unlock what's inside of you.

It cannot be avoided, it's something you must go through,

Then you're able to help others, who's hurting just like you.

It's so hard to see, past the pain it hurts so bad,

It stopped when I stopped; searching for something I already had.

Some may say they know, but I tell you, I've felt His glory,

I'll wait until He speaks to me after all this is His story.

I didn't ask for what came in life, it was handed down to me

Because I survived the madness, a new light shinning is what I see.

So, my journey has been rough, but I've learned a thing or two,

If it's one thing that shapes our life, it's the good that pain can do.

AND I HAVE YOU

Oceans have tides, Sun has shine,

Rivers have banks, you're forever mine.

Mountains have peaks, summer has fall,

Birds have wings, our love conquers all.

Eyes have sight, rain has drops,

Hearts have beats, for you mine never stops.

Boats have sails, sand has shores,

Beauty has looks that makes me yours.

Roses have thorns, days have nights,

The sky has stars in the twilight.

Jungles have lions, King and Queen

Salt has pepper, you and I have a team.

Valleys have hills, Bees have hives,

Butterflies have cocoons, husbands and wives.

Cupid has arrows, mist and dew,

Pepper has mint, and I have you.

SOMETHING NEW

Been running way too long from what's been chasing me,

Time to face this thing head on and set myself free.

I made a lot of promises in my heart I swore to keep,

When it came time to make a move, I couldn't take the leap.

I had to reassure myself to hang on with all I've got,

And if I run out of rope, grab a hold, and tie a knot.

For some, life's a guessing game, for you must find your niche,

There's no room left for error this time, throw the first pitch.

It's all been right in front of you, but you won't reach out and take it,

Time is slowly running out, it's now or you'll never make it.

You've waited longer than you wanted and now the stage is set,

You can't make up for lost time, but you can change tomorrow I bet.

You tried to stop, but follow the river whichever way it turned,

There's so much that you missed, so many things you never learned.

Now this is who you've become and the man you are to be,

No longer haunted by his past, no longer walking blindly.

No need to feel ashamed, all this was meant for you,

I stand in front of the same mirror, but today I see something new.

STEPPINGSTONE

The truth of the matter is there are no words to express,

How hard I made my bed, let me be the first to confess.

I've traveled many places, some I did not wish to go,

Been bounced back and forth each time the wind would blow.

If I could rewind the tape, a different song it would sing,

Out of all the bad, you finally see the good it brings.

It's difficult for most if you could just hold your ground,

And have a little faith that soon it will all turn around.

Because I know, I've made mistakes, but I have no regrets,

I know I must fight until it is no longer a threat.

It may look like a comeback is out of the question for sure,

You only stand to gain as much as you're willing to endure.

For those that put you down, said they did all they could do,

Never stop believing or pushing for a breakthrough.

I've shed my last tear, so I pick myself up off the floor,

And be careful not to step in the same holes I did once before.

It's okay to fall, but dust yourself off and be gone,

What used to be a stumbling block, is now a steppingstone.

IMAGINE

Imagine life on the other side how will it be,

Imagine yourself in heaven, what people would you see?

Imagine a ship lost at sea, amid a storms rage,

Imagine never growing old like a child that would never age.

Imagine if you were blind and suddenly could see,

Imagine being able to travel to the end of eternity.

Imagine a secret place when found couldn't be seen,

Imagine if everything you've lived has only been a dream.

Imagine a serene sky, violet, bright orange, and blue,

Imagine a future world where all things become new.

Imagine if the sun should one day fail to shine,

Imagine being taken away for good at such an unexpected time.

Imagine the deepest of loves that would never have to divide,

Imagine you searching the entire world but never stopping to look on the inside.

CARRY ME AWAY

Carry me away both high and far,

To a special place that's where you are.

Away from the hurt engraved in my heart,

Away from the troubles that's torn us apart.

Carry me off into a distant land,

Time and time again our love continues to stand.

The toils of life you and I will outshine,

We're unbeatable together, we're one of a kind.

Carry me through the storms of the sea,

What's left in the end shall always remain to be.

Carry me back when our love was strong and sure,

To carry on forward is required to make it pure.

Even the top of the sky could never be above,

What we share is more than perfect love.

Carry me past all my thoughts and cares,

Nothing that we face is more than we could bear.

Carry me in your heart and never face life alone,

Because we've stuck together our love will never roam.

To that special place we've gone there to stay,

It's forever in love my dear, that you carry me away.

FENCE I STRADDLED

I know we haven't talked in a while,

You say it was me cramping your style.

I hate that it ended the way that it did,

I see things different now, then I was just a kid.

When I didn't know any better it was all the same to me,

Sometimes the hard part is deciding what's meant to be.

But it cuts to the core and laces my heart with ache,

I had the best intentions, but it was too-little, too-late.

You see for me, to get better it was the rough times that were bad,

Sometimes you must lose what you got to realize what you had.

Now I'm sitting here thinking about what it is I'm missing,

The chance to make it right is still there I keep wishing.

After all this time I'm still wiping away the tears,

It's like looking at my reflection in a thousand broken mirrors.

Now I see why it was so hard for me to choose,

Trying so long to hold on to something I'm destined to lose.

I guess you thought it wasn't in me to overcome this battle,

I finally found the strength to lay down the fence I straddled.

THE BEST IS YET TO COME

I just can't seem to grasp the reality of what I see,

Sometimes my mind goes in reverse on its own uncontrollably.

I think about my life, my love, and how I found it,

Most lessons are learned through pain there's just no way around it.

Looking back now I wondered what was it all for?

Looking forward now I see it was to open a brand-new door.

I had what I thought was love, but it wasn't a sure thing,

If it survives, its purified, this kind of love is everlasting.

To walk this walk of faith is beyond you even though,

I realize that to hold on, you simply just have to let go.

A higher dimension of life is what we all dream of,

The most precious gift around is God's infinite love.

It's been said to forgive and forget, I know it's hard to do,

Try loving those that don't love back, Christ did it for me and you.

If you're tired of pretending step up and answer the call,

Stop playing games with your life and for once give it your all.

Remember you wanted to give up, they said you'd never make it,

It was your will that kept you going, they tried but couldn't break it.

Never let your past or where you come from

Get the best of you because, the best is yet to come.

RICHES MONEY CANNOT BUY

Have you ever questioned why things are going wrong?

You find yourself again just trying to hold on.

You've come to the end; you no longer can provide.

Every hope and every dream has gone away and died.

If I could only go back and change what I've done,

Most people don't believe in miracles until they need one.

There must be some reason, nothing happens by chance,

God does have a purpose for every circumstance.

With nothing to look forward to, sadness takes its place,

If you look deep enough within, you'll see the masters face.

I've experienced firsthand what it means to lose control,

I fought to save my life but now it's about my soul.

It's like planting a seed and waiting with enthusiasm,

It will flourish and spring up as deeply as you can fathom.

There will come a day when all the hurt is wiped away,

And that special place where even birds can't fly,

You'll find these riches even money cannot buy.

REACHING FOR THE TOP

All in all, I guess this is it, the old saying must be true,

If you play this game long enough it'll make a believer out of you.

I went around, came back, and yes, I had to go again,

This hand is fixed so no one can place bets to win.

If you're wondering why, you keep seeing that same old same old,

Stop looking at the glitter in life and find the path made of gold.

If it's behind, you let it go that's why it's the past,

Reach for immaterial things this is what will last.

After all the trial and error, you know there's just one way,

You may have missed your mark, but your tracks are here to stay.

If I could look a little deeper into my life, what would I see?

Someone dying to live but was trapped inside of me.

I've come way too far to go back on what I've pledged

To stand on firm ground instead of living on the edge.

You've never been any closer you're just a skip and a hop,

When you settle for good enough, you stop reaching for the top.

NOTHING TO LOSE

I've been through this maze before there wasn't any light,

I thought I was looking for answers to somehow make this right.

It doesn't make any sense that all this could take place,

Seems like everything I've done until now has been a waste.

I trusted and believed I had changed to make it better,

Why am I still standing out in the rain getting wetter?

A broken heart mends but what's a life of shattered dreams,

Watching it all slip through your fingers and starting over it seems.

It's not such a bad thing if you take it to heart,

You could paint your very own masterpiece, your own work of art.

Forget what people say or think just keep your head high,

And know that you can do it just spread your wings and fly.

Regardless of how you feel it will work out for the good,

Always believe in yourself you've always known you could.

If it's one thing for certain, no doubt you've had to suffer,

God knew you needed strength, so He sent this to make you tougher.

So, it is what it is, what more can I say,

After all these years I finally found a better way.

They say it's black or white this time I get to choose,

How could this not work with one chance left and nothing to lose?

HAPPINESS

If only I could have picked the road I would follow,

The facts of life wouldn't be so hard for me to swallow.

You win some you lose some I guess that's how it goes,

The highs we take in stride as we do with the lows.

To constantly feel like you're not at your best,

Seeking real companionship in our lives is a test.

Everything that goes up also must come down,

You get what you give it comes right back around.

Searching to find out what and who we really are,

Our sincerest desire to achieve was now a distant star.

To at last feel an inner push to reach for our goals,

A great deal of uncertainty is what the future holds.

Yesterday is spent and tomorrow is merely a vision,

The hardest thing to do is sometimes the best decision.

With the bad comes good we smile, and we laugh,

Happiness depends on what you are, not on what you have.

CROSSROAD

It's a known fact that life teaches us the hard way,

Everything you ever did wrong there's a price you have to pay.

We can dig for an explanation and ask for a reason why,

At times it hurts so bad you could just lie down and die.

Tell me it's not true, it's just a fairy tale,

Why this life I live, is like I'm trapped in a living hell.

Once you become aware you can no longer say you didn't know,

Plus, there are many people waiting to say, "I told you so".

I thought I was in the clear as it all came crashing down,

It crushed the very life in me I couldn't make a sound.

I still can't understand why I continue to play the fool,

It changes when we start to use what we learned as a tool.

Insensitive to the numbness of what I've lost and sacrificed,

He said if you gave it up for His sake one day, He'd see you in paradise.

At this moment, I surrender I can't go on another step,

You can't reach the highest high until you've hit the lowest depth.

There's nothing new under the sun, even this legend has been told,

If there's a fork dividing your street, straight ahead is the crossroad.

NOW I KNOW

Now I know why all this had to come about,

Instead of going within I was content going without.

Now I see why for me it took so much,

Wished I would've felt it with one simple touch.

Now I know it's not what's left to do but how far you've come,

Sometimes before you can get more you got to give some.

My dilemmas that have come and passed by,

Only because I stretched out my hands to the sky.

Now I know the decisions that I've made,

Caused me to weep but sharpened me like a blade.

I've stood under the pressure for some time now you see,

It's not rubies or even pearls this is how diamonds come to be.

Now I know that when you do find love,

If it makes it through the fire, you know what it's made of.

If indeed you've learned and have paid the price,

You can throw it all away with one roll of the dice.

Now I know how I was always at odds,

I couldn't quite put it together, so I kept blaming God.

So, I'm left trying to hide this face behind the show,

It's okay to remove the mask, because now I know.

THIS THING CALLED LIFE

I wonder what would happen if you had all you willed,

Could you see over the mountain without having climbed the hill?

If only I could see then, what I see now, to be true,

It wouldn't be so hard to accept or this so hard to do.

There's really no excuse, you reap what you sow,

And everything you endure is only to help you grow.

We sometimes need proof, so we keep doing things our way,

The people that love you most stop trying, turn, and look away.

Life can be funny trying to determine to who and what to give,

It's only when you stop being selfish you learn how to live.

When you feel there's, nothing left and the tides have turned,

That's when it hits the hardest all the bridges that you burned.

I didn't think I could be here back where I was before,

This time walking alone, the same people aren't there anymore.

It dawns on at once, you gambled and lost the deal,

You forfeit your hand each time you spin the wheel.

There's one thing I vow and that is to succeed,

Keep stepping until I make it for this my heart bleeds.

I can't turn back the hands or take away the strife,

To go on, I must get a grip on this thing called life.

YOUR REFLECTIVE THOUGHTS

ABOUT THE AUTHOR

Kenneth James, prolific orator and creator of musical lyrics, poetry, and soul-searching expositions that leave audiences profoundly breathless. Hailing from the South Suburbs of Chicago, Kenneth is the middle of eight children born to Willie and Pearl James.

Graduating from Hillcrest High School, attending Kankakee Community College & University of Wisconsin –La Crosse, Kenneth majored in computer science; but was most known for his true agility on the basketball court. Never one to shy away from a pick & roll, fade-away or slam dunk – Michael Jordan style - Kenneth is a true baller.

Throughout the years of his personal and professional experiences; *it can be surmised that Kenneth did not anticipate being used in ministry – he sought God and got apprehended.*

Kenneth has often said: "The heart of every problem is a problem of the heart. It's better to have a heart without words than words without a heart. Turn your disappointments into HIS appointments and watch God work on your behalf. God has never broken any promise ever spoken. It's not how you start things; it's how you finish."

It could be said that some people have the same declaration about life, while others vary. It can be sweet, aromatic, and fulfilling or it can mundane, repetitively exhaustive, or just plain discouraging. If your only concern is what you acquire in this world only, you have lost sight of what your true purpose is. Purpose is the reason for which something is done, created or for which something exists. Your existence permeates your purpose. For everything, there is a purpose. Not my will Lord, but Thy will be done.

If you are reading this book, my prayer would be that even in your darkest moments – you will search for truth. In times of sorrow, there is hope for your tomorrow. In your hour of despair, you are not alone, your burden He shares. The most important things in life don't always stand out; they are waiting for you to speak out. Speak those things that be not as though they were, (Roman 4:17) Sayeth the Lord.

Milton Keynes UK
Ingram Content Group UK Ltd.
UKHW020618050324
438776UK00006B/937